CONTENTS

	PAGE
Foreword	1

CHAPTER I—GENERAL CONSIDERATIONS

SEC
1. Introduction	1
2. Some aspects of fighting in built-up areas	2
3. Infantry weapons	7
4. Supporting arms and weapons	10
5. Equipment	12

CHAPTER II—ATTACK

6. Planning the attack	14
7. The main approaches	16
8. Conduct of the attack	18

CHAPTER III—DEFENCE

9. Organization of the defence	20
10. Conduct of the defence...	23

CHAPTER IV—MINOR TACTICS AND METHODS

11. Section drill for clearing a house	25
12. Platoon drill for clearing occupied houses	28
13. Defence of buildings	30
14. Siting of weapons	33
15. Do's and Don'ts	35

CHAPTER V—TRAINING

16. Object	37
17. Methods	37
18. Stages	38

APPENDICES

A. Protection Tables	39
B. Methods of scaling walls	39
C. Explosives	41
D. Plates	44

DISTRIBUTION

Infantry	Scale B
Other Arms	Scale A
OCTUs—Infantry	Scale IV
OCTUs—Other Arms	Scale II
Home Guard	6 copies per Bn.

> **NOT TO BE PUBLISHED**
>
> The information given in this document is not to be communicated, either directly or indirectly, to the Press or to any person not holding an official position in His Majesty's Service.

26/GS Publications/933

MILITARY TRAINING PAMPHLET
No. 55

FIGHTING IN BUILT-UP AREAS

1943

Crown Copyright Reserved

Prepared under the direction of
The Chief of the Imperial General Staff

THE WAR OFFICE,
April, 1943

The Naval & Military Press Ltd

Published by

The Naval & Military Press Ltd
Unit 5 Riverside, Brambleside
Bellbrook Industrial Estate
Uckfield, East Sussex
TN22 1QQ England

Tel: +44 (0)1825 749494

www.naval-military-press.com
www.nmarchive.com

*In reprinting in facsimile from the original, any imperfections are inevitably reproduced
and the quality may fall short of modern type and cartographic standards.*

FIGHTING IN BUILT-UP AREAS

MILITARY TRAINING PAMPHLET No. 55 1943

FOREWORD

The object of this pamphlet is to explain the nature of fighting in built-up areas and to give guidance on methods of exploiting their characteristics to the best advantage against modern enemies.

No attempt has been made to deal in detail with the approach to, or defence from, the outskirts of a built-up area, or with points of tactics and administration that are common to all forms of land warfare.

CHAPTER I—GENERAL CONSIDERATIONS

1. Introduction

1. Preparation for fighting in built-up areas must be considered an integral part of every soldier's training. Such fighting is not a job for the specialist. Much fighting in this war has revolved about, or taken place in, towns because of their value to modern armies as centres of communication.

2. The importance of the occupation and defence of urban areas is not confined to forward troops. So long as deep penetration by ground or airborne attack continues to be possible, the chief focal points within enemy reach must be defended. Troops of all arms must, therefore, be prepared to organize attack and defence in urban areas and know how to fight in the houses and streets.

3. It is generally accepted that built-up areas favour the defence. This view is borne out by the fact that the irregularities of pattern of the present-day battlefield are largely due to such areas being able to hold out while the attackers progress to considerable distances between and beyond them. Although this pamphlet deals with the various aspects of fighting in built-up areas, it is not intended to convey the impression that towns and villages are *ipso facto* the main props of a defensive organization. The defence of certain towns or villages may be dictated by their strategical value, but often the tactical results will be the loss of surprise and the provision of well defined and concentrated targets for the enemy. At any rate, success in dealing with the problems involved will only be attained by training and practice, and by the use of imagination on the part of all ranks.

2. Some aspects of fighting in built-up areas

4. The principles of town fighting differ in no way from those which govern more open warfare. There are, however, special circumstances attached to town fighting which have a direct bearing on the tactics employed.

5. The ground.—No other battlefield includes ground both so open and so close. In every street are coverless stretches affording ideal fields of fire. Bordering every street are numerous protected firing positions, hiding places, and sources of ambush. It follows that fighting will nearly always be at close quarters, casualties high, and the nerve strain for both sides heavy.

When a built-up area is the scene of a prolonged period of fighting, however, many of its characteristics will be modified. Buildings are liable to become heaps of rubble and fields of view thereby increased. When a whole sector of a town is reduced to rubble, the piles of debris render the area analogous to close country providing much cover; they will also restrict movement, except on foot. This possible change in the character of a built-up area must be borne in mind when reading this pamphlet, which deals with a built-up area in which most of the buildings are still standing.

6. Built-up areas are usually made up, apart from factories, parks, etc., of three distinct house arrangements: on the outskirts, isolated houses or groups of houses surrounded by gardens, trees, fields, and allotments; farther in, closely-spaced detached and semi-detached houses; and, nearest the centre, blocks of houses and large buildings.

7. In the area of isolated houses, buildings represent inferior pill boxes and should be treated as such in attack or defence. Detached and semi-detached jerry-built houses closely spaced are the intermediate stage and are usually flanked by streets on one side and small gardens or back areas on the other. The centre of a town almost invariably consists of buildings built on the block system, so that except for open squares, there is little or no space between them other than that essential for streets and alley-ways; but it is important to note that nearly all such buildings have cellars and basements, which assist the defence greatly.

8. In densely built-up areas it is possible to climb thirty, fifty, perhaps a hundred feet in as many seconds; it is possible to by-pass an enemy by going directly over or under him. Built-up areas thus possess a third dimension not present in open warfare which, combined with the abundance of cover, involves a constant drain on man power, creates

great difficulties of cohesion and control, and calls for a maximum of ingenuity from everyone engaged.

9. *Difficulty of control.*—Buildings cause exceptionally blind and disjointed conditions. In no other form of warfare, except in dense forest and bush, are there such narrow and limited horizons, or such physical barriers between units of the same force. Highly centralized control will be difficult ; most of the fighting will resolve itself into small independent actions, and much will depend upon individual initiative and capabilities. Distances will be short, and therefore will allow commanders to exert a more decisive influence in the local battle, because personal appearances well forward in their areas can be made more easily and more quickly than in other forms of fighting.

10. *Value of short-range weapons.*—Comparison with open warfare brings out the fact that there is a difference in the relative values of the various weapons. AFVs, aircraft, and artillery, though invaluable adjuncts, are restricted in their roles ; whereas short-range weapons and explosives predominate. Smoke assumes an added importance ; while the effect of noise, greatly increased on account of the enclosed nature of such areas, can be exploited to an extent out of all proportion to the effort required for its production. The psychological effect of noise and fire, especially by night, may often be exploited.

11. *Restricted visibility.*—Buildings obscure view, and visibility during actual fighting is apt further to be restricted on account of brick dust caused by the strike of projectiles and by explosive charges. Owing to the presence of buildings smoke tends to remain concentrated for longer periods than is normal.

Reconnaissance will not be effective by observation alone, and information will have to be gained by fighting, to induce the enemy to disclose his weapons and general dispositions.

12. *Conspicuousness of movement.*—Because the major part of cover is rigid and set out in straight lines, movement is easily seen. This rule applies especially to individual men, if they do not remain motionless when observing or firing from behind cover. Therefore small parties must always move well dispersed, from cover to cover, and always under the keen observation and ready fire support of their nearest neighbours.

13. *Difficulty of locating fire.*—The point of origin of fire is difficult to locate on account of the noise of discharge being drowned by the crack of a bullet as it passes or by the noise of impact of a projectile, and because of the bewildering number of points from which fire can be brought to bear in a relatively small area. It is also difficult to recognize and distinguish

between the noise of strike and the noise of discharge. Consequently, false rumours and information are apt to arise concerning such points as the presence of enemy snipers. What may sound like enemy firing from adjacent rooms or buildings may mean in reality that the latter are being subjected to fire from elsewhere. Such situations occur frequently when a house is being searched, and may cause such operations to be unduly slow.

14. *Restricted manœuvre.*—Manœuvre is restricted according to the density of buildings and the nakedness of streets. Success will depend largely upon the judicious variation of method ; at one moment stealth and cunning under a small tactical fire plan, at the next the impetus of brute force and speed, for which the qualities of physical fitness and determination to kill are as essential as in open field warfare.

15. *Value of the first shot.*—Fighting is at close quarters, and an aimed shot should be infallibly accurate. Neutralization of fire has, therefore, to be absolute, and covering fire is essential for the smallest operation. A single marksman left undisturbed may be able to prevent any small tactical operation.

16. The enemy's fire can be stopped by ours in two main ways : either by getting in the first shot, or by getting in more shots, and from more directions, than the enemy can. The first is preferable and saves valuable lives, but, to obtain it, observation by every man in an organized system must be taught.

17. *Darkness.*—Owing to the restriction of movement outside buildings by day much fighting in towns will take place at night. Streets can be crossed, small parties can stalk past defended houses, and it will be difficult to distinguish between friend and foe. Darkness is the ally of the attacker rather than of the defence.

18. *Fire (the element).*—Fire can be a formidable and disconcerting agent and is a potent factor in town fighting. A German manual states that " the burning of houses will hasten success," and it is indeed obvious that situations will arise in which the quickest, surest, most economical, and perhaps the only way of dislodging the enemy from a building will be by burning it. In defence, precautions against fire should be given high priority to ensure that the work of fortifying buildings is not undone by the first incendiary projectile.

19. Used intentionally, fire produced by one's own side has a very heartening influence and a proportionately depressing effect upon the enemy. Nevertheless, clear orders concerning the use of incendiarism are always necessary, because it is a double-edged weapon, which can do more harm than good.

20. *Looting.*—The ordinary battlefield offers few amenities calculated to distract a soldier ; a built-up area, unless completely devastated, offers many. The acquisition of loot is likely to lead to the discarding of equipment, with a resultant loss of efficiency. However well disciplined a unit may be, looting will, unless precautions are taken in advance, begin on a small scale and tend to increase. It stops progress, deteriorates the soldier, and must be heavily punished.

21. *Importance of height.*—The possession of height gives a feeling of security over an enemy who is on a lower level, but is often counterbalanced by the effect of hostile air-bombing, which will generally accompany the attack or defence of urban areas.

The defender, who has usually had time to conceal and protect his fire points and to guard all approaches to his level from heights above, will usually prefer to employ his fire raking the streets and lower storeys, feeling that if buildings collapse from shelling and bombing, the rubble, etc., will strengthen his cover and block the streets, thereby giving him increased security and better targets. The attacker, however, will require height to act as depth to his fire support and to assist his observation. The defender knows this fact and will arrange to meet it. The use of available high buildings may, against a well-equipped army, prove over-expensive except for sniper and observation posts ; and better progress in the attack and greater effect of fire in the defence may be produced by action in and through lower storeys and basements. The shape of roofs and the facilities for reaching them are very important factors in these considerations.

22. **Civilians.**—The problems of controlling and administering the civilian inhabitants will nearly always arise, and may be complicated by a flow of refugees into built-up areas and by fifth columnists. The degree of assistance and co-operation that may be expected from the civilian inhabitants will vary greatly. At one extreme is the full co-operation of inhabitants of a home town in the event of an invasion of this country. In an invasion of the continent there would be friendly and unfriendly elements in most cities of the enemy-occupied countries. In operations in an enemy country itself, the population will inevitably be hostile.

In the last instance little in the way of co-operation can be achieved, but, wherever there are friendly elements the maximum assistance should be obtained from them.

23. In defence, if total evacuation be ordered, many of the public services useful to the organization of defence will cease. It will be necessary to feed and accommodate those civilians not evacuated, at the same time ensuring that evacuated civilians cannot be usefully employed, even against their will, by the enemy. If evacuation is inadvisable, it will be normal to segregate civilians, or at least women and children, into particular parts of a town. In attack, non-essential civilians should be evacuated as soon as possible from important areas as soon as these are gained.

24. Dealing with civilians is one of the most difficult problems connected with fighting in built-up areas, and great strictness must be exercised to keep out spies and fifth columnists. In the defence or occupation of a town, the services of any civilians who can assist the military will, of course, be utilized to the fullest extent—e.g., doctors, food suppliers, distributors, nurses, representatives of the local government, and public utility services. It may be necessary to grant special treatment or facilities for movement to some or all of these ; passes of different colours may be necessary. Liaison between civil and military authorities must be arranged and practised.

25. The control of civilians will in any event require constant attention, and arrangements should be made for sudden unforeseen movement either into an area or out of it. Bombing will tend to drive the inhabitants out of a town, while the ground action on the outskirts that follows will drive them in again.

26. *Summary.*—Fighting in built-up areas reduces the advantages enjoyed in open warfare by the side that is superior in mobile equipment and vehicles ; it involves chiefly infantry action, in the form of small, numerous, and independent battles ; and its dominant feature is an abundance of cover interspersed with short, open fields of fire. Such fighting, therefore, favours the defence, except possibly at night. In addition, it requires increased man power for a given area. Above all, because of the enclosed nature of the fighting, success depends on the determination, cunning, and trained observation of the individual. Heavy shelling and air bombing at the right place and time may be more decisive in built-up areas than in the field.

3. Infantry weapons

A. Field Force

27. *The rifle* in practised hands is an immensely valuable and reliable weapon. At the necessarily short ranges, inaccurate fire should never occur. The rifle is sometimes described as cumbersome in streets and houses—but never by men who are used to its manipulation and to carrying it.

Effective sniping in an enclosed area can, by itself, bewilder and almost paralyse the efforts of the other side.

28. *LMGs* are the main supporting weapons in the attack and should not normally be carried into the actual assault, since they are too heavy and bulky for hand-to-hand fighting. They are invaluable for covering streets and open spaces and for "swamping" enemy covering fire. Normally in defence a large proportion should be used from a low level to obtain full grazing effect from their beaten zone, and for covering short open stretches which can be rushed. In attack a flat beaten zone will not always be required to the same extent; most of the LMGs available should be sited high up in buildings, in order to fire downwards into windows or rooftops and to give covering fire to an assault until the last possible moment.

29. *The machine carbine* is an ideal weapon for hand-to-hand fighting and affords the main reserve of fire power literally in the hands of each section commander. It has, however, small powers of penetration and, contrary to general belief, is ineffective against bolts and locks of doors.

30. *The anti-tank rifle* is too heavy and unwieldy for close combat. It is useful for driving a sniper out of light cover, and for use against light tanks and guns brought up to point blank range, or against soft vehicles. Normally, however, it will pay to carry, especially in attack, projectors or dischargers with a superior all-round performance.

31. *The 2-inch mortar* is very effective as a smoke projector. The HE bomb will not penetrate buildings, but can be used, particularly in defence, for harassing effect. The HE bomb from a 2-inch mortar, skilfully handled, is useful for firing into back gardens and reaching the enemy in similar enclosed types of cover. When smoke is required at short ranges up a street, the bomb can be projected at a low angle against the side walls formed by the houses. Such projection will cause it to ricochet into the road and prevent it going too far.

32. *The 3-inch mortar.*—The use of this weapon is limited because it cannot fire at ranges below 250 yards and the HE

bomb with its instantaneous fuze has no penetrative power against houses. It is useful for producing a heavy concentration of HE in a short period for harassing effect, and is effective for the engagement of bombed-out areas, in which the roofs have been destroyed. (*See* Plate 8.)

33. *Projectors or the discharger cup and rifle* should be carried by leading sections in the attack. The No. 68 grenade or equivalent may be useful for penetrating walls or doors at short range, while the No. 36 grenade can be projected through windows out of range of hand throwers. The effect of a No. 68 or similar grenade is to blast a relatively small hole. To gain entry into a house, it may be necessary to fire several shots to enlarge the area of the hole, or else to knock in the loose bricks or masonry by hand.

34. *The No. 36 grenade* may be used for rolling downstairs and into cellars or dropping down chimneys, for throwing through open doors, windows, or holes in a wall, and for setting up booby traps. The fact that it has a time fuze should be thoroughly understood by those who use it. It will not breach doors or walls.

35. *The No. 69 grenade* is small and light and is useful in the final stages of an assault. It is not a killer, and is useful chiefly for its moral effect. It must be followed up immediately.

36. *The No. 74 grenade* provides a rapid and effective means of breaching the stoutest door and brick walls, particularly if used in pairs (one undetonated smashed against the wall, and the second planted against it and set off in the normal manner). These grenades are not effective against well-made, stone-built houses. (*See* Appendix C.)

37. *The No. 75 grenade (Hawkins)* provides a rapidly made tank or vehicle obstacle, or booby trap; it is easy to conceal in the debris that is likely to litter the streets. It is effective for breaching walls when used as a pole charge. (*See* Appendix C.)

38. *The SIP grenade* may be invaluable both against tanks and vehicles, for setting fire to houses when used against inflammable material, and for providing smoke screens. The glass containers will not normally break when thrown through a window or into a room; they are then more effective if coupled with a detonator and time fuze.

39. *Smoke grenades.*—The importance of smoke, both to provide concealment and to distract the enemy, is so great that a liberal supply will always be required.

40. *Anti-tank guns* should be used against tanks chiefly to cover streets, barricades, and open spaces from suitably defiladed positions. The solid shot will penetrate one or more walls, leaving a relatively small hole. An anti-tank gun can be used, therefore, to destroy a sniper behind cover, to harass the occupants of a building with a view to forcing them to leave it, or to destroy a section of a house or road block by repeated shots. Used in such a role it can be easily spotted ; it should therefore be brought into action for short periods only, and its position should be frequently changed.

The accuracy is such that successive shots aimed at the same spot go through the same hole and cumulative penetration is achieved. This would be very effective against a small strong point, but against a large house, block of flats, etc, where it is not possible to pin-point the defence, it would be relatively ineffective. The solid shot has a drilling effect only, and a very large number of shots would be required to destroy a section of a house.

41. *The pistol*, in practised hands, is a useful weapon for very close-quarter fighting, as when searching a house. In unskilful hands the weapon is more likely to disconcert, if not actually endanger our own troops than to damage the enemy.

B. Home Guard

42. Apart from the weapons common to the field force and the Home Guard, the latter are equipped with a number of weapons particularly useful for town fighting.

43. *Shot guns*, being light in weight and quick to fire, are useful weapons for close combat. At short ranges their lethal effect is great.

44. *The ·22-inch rifle* is not to be despised. In the hands of a good shot it can be very useful for sniping purposes. It is easily concealed, and a pocketful of ammunition will last for days.

45. *The Northover projector* is a useful weapon for putting No. 36 grenades through distant windows, for setting alight inflammable targets when firing the SIP grenade, or for breaching doors or brick walls with the No. 68 grenade.

46. *The spigot mortar* with its anti-tank bomb will breach almost any wall, while its anti-personnel bomb can be used more effectively than the 3-inch mortar HE bomb. Its comparative immobility makes it unsuitable in attack.

47. *The Smith gun*, although not as destructive as the spigot mortar, is mobile and has good powers of breaching

walls; it is useful for the engagement of AFVs. When using the 8 lb HE bomb against walls, oblique fire will give the best results.

4. Supporting arms and weapons

48. MMGs.—In good visibility they compare unfavourably with LMGs, as they are more difficult to conceal and handle. They should be used chiefly to cover open spaces outside the perimeter of a built-up area, or to fire in enfilade down long streets. On account of their rapid and sustained fire they may occasionally be used for sweeping roof tops and for their harassing effect.

At night or in smoke they are useful for firing on fixed lines directed at barricades or along streets.

49. AFVs.—Tanks and armoured cars suffer from certain disadvantages in towns since their movement is limited to narrow defiles. It is difficult for them either to locate an enemy or bolt him from cover; they lay themselves open to ambushes, and can be attacked from levels above and below those which their weapons can reach.

Nevertheless their armour and weapons can on some occasions be used with great effect. Against a hastily organized or unprepared defence, the bold employment of AFVs may enable an area to be overrun more quickly and with less cost than by the use of infantry alone. Against a determined and organized enemy, whether in attack or defence, their chief role will be to help in the reduction of enemy posts and strong points by using their heavier weapons. It will be the task of the infantry and artillery to neutralize anti-tank weapons, to help AFVs to manœuvre into position using smoke, to reconnoitre and make diversions, and to provide guides and escorts. Once in position, because of the short ranges involved, AFVs should be able to command a short length of street and put out of action any anti-tank weapon while the latter is being brought into position.

On some occasions, crash action by tanks into a house may be effective in making an entrance for infantry.

50. Field, medium and heavy artillery.—After the initial phases of an attack on a town, artillery action by both sides will be limited in scope.

During the attack, concentrations, especially by the heavier natures of guns, may be fired on prominent buildings from outside the perimeter, and harassing fire will be on a big scale by day and night. Forward limits of our own troops will, however, be difficult to define. Field artillery may also be used over open sights for the reduction of enemy strong points, and special provision of extra armour piercing ammunition will normally be advisable.

In the defence, once the enemy is established in the town, field artillery may continue to be used against known enemy lines of approach to the town ; it may be given an anti-tank role from defiladed positions ; or used firing over open sights, to eject enemy from buildings.

51. *Anti-tank artillery* in principle is used for the same roles as the infantry anti-tank gun. Anti-tank regiments may, however, sometimes be armed with a weapon of better performance. When possible, field guns and even medium artillery should be used in similar roles. Their destructive powers amongst buildings is very great.

52. **Engineers.**—In general the duties and methods of employment of engineers will not differ from those in other types of operations.

53. During an attack they should be used as part of the actual assault troops only when the rapid removal of mines or the use of demolitions or explosives is necessary and is beyond the scope of other arms. RE personnel will be required to follow up an assault in order to remove booby traps, carry out major defensive preparations in captured buildings, demolish buildings that are liable to collapse, and to improve communications.

54. In defence, they will be especially useful in the preparatory stages when engineer resources and the variety of expedients will normally be plentiful. Probable tasks will be the defensive preparation or structural improvement of important headquarters and installations, work on road blocks and communications, the setting up of booby traps, laying charges for cratering, and the more elaborate measures for deception.

55. Other duties may include sapping ; the production of explosive and demolition charges designed for special use by other arms, and the conversion of available material for specific purposes.

56. **Flame-throwers.**—The moral effect of flame-throwers is great ; full use should therefore be made of them when available. The man-pack flame-thrower capable of throwing a jet 25 to 30 yards will, when available for such operations, be extremely useful in attack for setting buildings on fire, burning barricades, and playing on well-protected windows and loopholes. An additional use in defence will be the engagement of enemy infantry and vehicles from windows. If a

tank can first be immobilized by blocks or other means, the flame-thrower will be a useful tank-hunting weapon in attack or defence.

57. The man-pack flame-thrower provides a very effective additional weapon when entering and clearing houses. A jet or two of liquid flame before the ascent of a staircase, the entry of a room, or the turning of an awkward corner inside a house will do much to neutralize possible resistance. The man-pack flame-thrower cannot, however, accompany the first party to effect an entry, because the bulkiness of the equipment reduces considerably the wearer's mobility, and reasonable access through a door or a window must first of all be assured to him. One man armed with a machine-carbine must be detailed as personal bodyguard to the flame-thrower operator.

58. **Aircraft.**—Reconnaissance from the air will have reduced value, since the majority of the forces engaged will be permanently under cover. As communications for ground forces will be difficult, reconnaissance aircraft may be used for locating the positions of forward troops by means of recognition signals displayed in the streets or on roof tops.

Preliminary photographic reconnaissance of towns to supplement street maps will be of great value. (*See* Plates 7, 8, and 11.)

59. Towns provide ideal targets for bombing. Considerable numbers of the enemy are likely to be immobilized after bombing, for a period that will depend on its intensity.

Once both sides are in occupation of parts of a town, the definition of the bomb line will be difficult and will greatly restrict the use of bombs. A thoroughly bombed town is most difficult to penetrate, because the debris provides protection and concealment for the weapons of the defence.

5. Equipment

60. Town fighting requires quick and agile movement. A reduction in the standard equipment carried must always, therefore, be considered, especially if men are to carry special weapons.

61. The following modifications to normal scales are amongst those which should be considered:—

(a) Even if gas has been used, it may be justifiable to discard the *anti-gas respirator*, though it is useful in smoke. A commander must balance the handicap to the fighting efficiency of his troops against the risk entailed. More often it will be safe to withdraw the *anti-gas cape*, since it is improbable that the enemy will use gas spray when in close contact with our troops in a built-up area.

(b) *Ammunition boots* are noisy and cumbersome for agile movement along pavements and roads and in houses; they hinder climbing. Some other form of foot wear, e.g., rubber or rope-soled shoes, or gum boots, will often be advisable, when available, especially for patrols. Failing other means, sandbags, towels, etc., tied round boots help to deaden noise.

(c) *The haversack*, when worn on the back, is conspicuous on a lying or crawling man and impedes his movement when crawling through narrow openings. It will often be more convenient for the man to wear it at the side, using it as an additional container for grenades, demolition equipment, etc.

(d) *Picks or crowbars* are necessary, whether in attack or defence, for smashing doors, levering up floor boards, and making holes through walls. A section requires at least one of each.

(e) *Torches and candles* may be essential. Torches should be dimmed, unless required as searchlights, and have narrow beams.

(f) *Chalk* is useful for writing instructions on walls to succeeding units, and for directing runners, marking HQs, etc.

(g) *Ladders* may be required for scaling walls and entering upper windows, but are cumbersome. The light scaling ladder for backyard movement may be most useful, especially in the first rush.

(h) *Fish line* or strong string will be useful in many ways, e.g., setting up booby traps and trip wires, pulling stores or SAA up to top floors.

(i) *Lengths of rope* with toggle and eye will enable both individual men and parties to scale walls, and have the advantage of being light and easily carried.

(j) *Explosives* will be required for many purposes. Appendix C deals with their use.

(k) *Periscopes.* Even home-made productions or single reflecting mirrors will be of value for observing from under cover.

(l) *Flags, signs, etc.* Some means will be necessary to show which houses are occupied by our troops in areas of close contact with the enemy.

(m) *Fire fighting equipment.* Essential for defence and valuable in attack.

(n) *Field glasses* are often the only means whereby a sniper or post can be located.

(o) *Grappling irons* are easily made and, if designed with an eye, can be fastened to ropes for the purpose of scaling walls and entering first-floor windows. A " bite " of as little as half an inch on a good piece of brickwork or wood will take a man's weight.

Many of the above and other valuable articles may often be found in the town itself. All men should be taught what to look for in this respect and to inform their NCOs.

CHAPTER II—ATTACK

6. Planning the attack

62. There is seldom a clearly defined boundary between town and country. Nearly every town is surrounded by a suburban area, which is frequently further extended by a ribbon development of buildings along the approaches to the town. (*See* Plates 1–4.)

It will usually be convenient to plan the attack in three main phases :—

(a) Gaining a footing in the town proper.

(b) Progression within the town.

(c) Reduction of individual centres of resistance.

63. **Gaining a footing.**—The first phase is not the subject of this pamphlet and only the broad principles need be mentioned. They are as follows :—

(a) A footing should be gained on as wide a front as possible in order to mislead the enemy and to secure the greatest number of jumping-off points for the second phase.

(b) Maximum artillery and air support will be required. Likely enemy OPs should be neutralized ; while the maximum destruction by bombing, particularly with incendiary bombs, will immobilize a proportion of the defenders by compelling their employment on clearing streets, rescue work, and fire fighting.

(c) The cover of darkness should be fully exploited.

(d) Centres of resistance should be avoided if they cannot be neutralized.

(e) Objectives should include those areas most effective for the second phase.

64. **Progression within a built-up area.**—Where the forces available in relation to the size of the town permit, it will often be best to stage a frontal attack in conjunction with a gradual double envelopment of the flanks. With smaller forces three main alternatives are open to the attackers for the second phase :—
- (a) *To penetrate along converging axes*, on narrow fronts, from a number of points on the perimeter with the object of seizing vital centres ; the occupation of the latter will disrupt the defence and allow expansion towards the rear of the perimeter defences.
- (b) *To advance on a broader front*, with the object of systematically *encroaching* into one area of the town at a time.
- (c) To attack on a *concentrated and narrow frontage* along one axis at a time with a view to cutting off, or dividing, a part of the defences. Resistance within an area so isolated should be overcome before a further attack is mounted.

65. The first and third methods depend upon the ability to probe deep into the defences between the main centres of resistance, and require sufficient numbers continually to extend the attack and relieve forward troops at each intermediate objective. The first method is therefore more likely to succeed against a hastily organized or unaggressive defence. The third method, although more systematic and probably slower, enables the attack to be concentrated along one axis at a time. Provided that the axis is not too rigid in its direction, this method can be employed with success against the strongest defence.

In every attack, objectives should be given that are clearly recognizable as rallying points. Advanced troops will employ infiltration tactics the more boldly if they know exactly how far they are to go.

66. *Reduction of centres of resistance*.—The final phase will be the reduction of centres which are still resisting, especially those that have been by-passed during the second phase.

67. *Cordons*.—When the object of an attack is to isolate or systematically to over-run an area, it will be necessary to cordon the flanks to prevent enemy movement into or out of that area.

68. When the object is **penetration** to selected centres or rallying points, cordoning **along the** routes may be required, to prevent the head of the att**ack** being cut off and to maintain communications.

69. Cordoning should be carried out by fire as much as possible in order to save man-power.

7. The main approaches

70. **Types.**—Whichever main form of attack is used, the attacker will have the choice of some or all of the five following routes of approach, which may be used separately or in combination :—

(a) Streets.

(b) Back yards or gardens behind houses and parallel to streets.

(c) Roofs of houses.

(d) Inside houses through the walls dividing them.

(e) Underground approaches.

71. *Movement along streets.*—A street may present an almost coverless defile, liable to ambush at any point. Its main advantage is then that it makes for speed and affords the possibility of a quick decision when the defence is not well organized. Movement along a main street also permits the use of tanks, with MG support from neighbouring windows and perhaps from a field gun from a corner or porch. In every such operation, small active groups must be prepared to operate on both flanks, along side streets and back yards, in order to outflank at once any building that presents a difficulty.

72. The greater part of the fighting in towns does not take place in the streets; it takes place in the alley ways, the back gardens, and in the houses themselves. Nevertheless, until resistance is met, the open streets provide the quickest means of advance.

73. The advance should be made along both sides of the street, individuals keeping as close as possible to houses, railings, or walls, and covering the houses on the opposite side of the street. As he advances, each individual should be continually selecting a piece of cover, behind or into which he can move the instant he is fired upon, and watching for snipers, machine guns, etc. ahead, on the opposite side of the street, especially in corner houses.

74. When smoke is used, the screen must be dense; otherwise it will tend to obscure the defenders—already presumably well concealed—from the attackers, whilst leaving the latter still visible.

75. Such covering fire as is possible must be arranged at the entrance to the street and, as the advance progresses, from

points along the street. It should be given from a sufficient height above the advancing troops to allow fire to continue up to the last possible moment, and, whenever possible, it should be so directed as to fire down into occupied windows rather than upwards.

76. *Advancing by back areas of houses.*—This method resembles that of advancing along streets, but has the advantage of providing more cover during movement. To obtain maximum concealment it is better to break through fences than to climb over them, unless smoke is used. Covering fire into the cover behind the houses, as well as against the houses themselves, must be arranged. Anti-tank guns, pulled by dragropes, and mortars are invaluable in these circumstances.

77. *Advancing along roof-tops.*—An attacker crawling under cover of the parapet along the roofs of a continuous block of buildings may have excellent cover, not only from the ground or windows occupied by the enemy, but also from snipers on other roofs. Usually flat roof-tops are the easiest to advance along and have better parapets, but ridged roofs are defiladed from one side and this fact must be exploited.

78. *Advancing through houses.*—The attacker may gain a footing in the first house of a block or, while advancing down a street or along the backs of houses, he may be forced into a house for protection. Advancing through houses will necessarily be slow because of the difficulties of forcing an entrance from one house to the next and the possible need for overcoming opposition at very close quarters. But protection from view and fire is more continuous, and the method provides immediate cover against enemy counter-attacks. A field gun can often be dragged into the first of a row of houses. Its fire will soon demolish several walls, after which grenades and flame-throwers may quickly clear out the defenders.

79. *Advancing by underground approaches.*—On rare occasions penetration and surprise may be achieved by the use of suitable subterranean passages or tunnels. These are seldom available except when sewers, underground railways, or canal tunnels exist. Their chief dangers are gases, flooding, and the ease with which they can be enfiladed or blocked. They should be considered for use in attack against a hastily prepared defence ; guides may be required.

80. **Booby traps.**—The enemy may use booby traps with the object of imposing caution on the attackers and creating an atmosphere of uncertainty, thereby lowering morale and slowing down progress. Detection is an all arms responsibility,

but booby traps will be removed only by trained personnel. All ranks should have some knowledge of what to look out for and what to avoid ; suspicious localities should, if possible, be by-passed and reported for examination later.

Booby traps are of two main types—those which are actuated by some movement or act of the attackers, and those which work by a time mechanism. The former type will best be avoided by refraining from touching any suspicious object found lying about, though there are types operated by such necessary acts as treading on a board or opening a door or window. The latter type are difficult to detect. Delay mechanisms are manufactured with fixed delays of anything from one hour to 28 days. Both types might be detected by such traces as marks on floors, walls, or elsewhere without an obvious reason ; the presence of pegs, nails, or small movable objects—even souvenirs—without any apparent reason ; freshly-placed heaps of shavings, etc.; or minor obstructions.

It is important to keep a balanced mind in this matter : instruction and demonstration beforehand will best achieve this result ; the main point to emphasize is that elaborate booby traps are unlikely to be found in houses which the enemy is actually occupying or has very recently been occupying for defence purposes.

8. Conduct of the attack

81. *Control.*—It is essential that the planning of a deliberate attack should be meticulous and methodical and that nothing should be left to chance. Dispersion and disruption are difficult to avoid in a mass of buildings and side streets ; control, once lost, is not easy to regain. It follows, therefore, that objectives must be limited and clearly defined, and that frontages must be reduced to allow successive units or sub-units to take over at frequent intervals, thus maintaining momentum. Units passing through must be kept under observation and fire support by those passed through.

Control will be facilitated if the axes of attack follow the main thoroughfares and not the side streets, but a commander must balance this advantage against the disadvantage that enemy resistance will probably be greatest astride the main thoroughfares.

It is essential to establish report centres as an attack progresses, and to make their location known to all ranks of the attackers.

82. *Covering fire.*—It is axiomatic that all movement, even by individuals in their sub-units, in the presence of the enemy must be covered by fire. Care is needed to guard against the premature disclosure of the position from which covering fire is to be given.

83. *Supporting arms.*—Concealment can be obtained as far forward as the leading elements ; consequently a proportion of such supporting arms and weapons as may be allotted should follow up each stage of an attack closely. Commanders of supporting arms, or their subordinates, should move by bounds, close up to the leading infantry sub-units. They will so allow engineers, AFVs, and guns—the latter for direct fire—to operate with the minimum delay. Guns may well be employed by sections, guns leap-frogging each other ; one gun will thus be in action all the time.

84. Supporting arms will normally be decentralized considerably to allow of their use to the best advantage in the various small independent battles that will result.

85. **Tanks.**—The enemy will seldom be in a position to command every street or approach with anti-tank weapons, neither will he be able to use them with full effect because of the covering fire, including smoke or other expedients, that will be employed against him. Consequently, there will be many occasions when tanks can be used in small numbers with success and when the hazards that they may meet will certainly be no greater than those met by the infantry. They should be regarded as self-propelled armoured guns rather than as armoured vehicles possessing ability to manœuvre across country.

86. It will be the responsibility of infantry to reconnoitre for tanks, to locate opposition, and to act as escort ; to provide close defence against hand-thrown grenades and to give covering fire from positions on the ground, in second storeys, and on the tops of buildings. Tank crews can see and engage targets at the lower levels, the infantry dealing with enemy higher up, including those on roofs.

87. The infantry will normally lead the attack and ensure that tanks are not ambushed. The leading tanks should follow up closely in short bounds, prepared to blast enemy resistance out of the way as soon as it has been located.

88. When enemy resistance has been hastily organized or it is suspected that his anti-tank resources are small, success may be obtained more rapidly and at less cost if tanks are used boldly and lead the infantry against successive short objectives. It is imperative that infantry should follow at best speed ; they must always be within supporting distance and must quickly relieve the tanks at each intermediate objective.

89. Smoke will frequently be of great assistance but, when used, it must be placed well away from the tanks and as near the points of origin of enemy fire as possible.

90. The use of long range flame-throwers installed in tanks or carriers will be effective in neutralizing enemy resistance and possibly in driving the enemy out of cover, but the risk will remain of buildings being set alight, especially if furnished. If flame-throwers are used, particular care is necessary to ensure the safety of infantrymen on foot.

91. It will rarely be possible for tanks to be used in force to co-operate with infantry in the normal manner, but when so employed they should be divided into echelons according to tasks required. For example, they may be divided into three echelons : the first to provide close support for assaulting infantry ; the second to help to clear up centres of resistance that have been by-passed ; and the third to engage immediate enemy counter-attacks delivered in rear of the assaulting troops.

CHAPTER III—DEFENCE

9. Organization of the defence

92. As in any other form of defence, section and platoon posts will be grouped to form defended localities, which may in turn be organized as components of a larger defended area.

93. An ideal layout for the all-round defence of a small built-up area might be to man the perimeter in sufficient strength to prevent enemy infiltration ; to have a system of mutually defended strongpoints sited in concentric rings from the perimeter to the centre of the area ; to have mobile reserves sited at various points for immediate local counter-attacks ; and in the centre a strong keep, in or near which are located the commander's main reserves. The strength of a garrison will dictate defensive details, but reserves for counter-attacks must be as strong as possible.

In the smallest types of built-up areas, such as villages or hamlets, this type of layout is possible because the perimeter is short and the central keep or reserve sufficiently close to provide depth and immediate support to any point on it.

94. Such a layout is in larger areas obviously impracticable. A town with a total area of one square mile has a perimeter of approximately four miles, and the area enclosed by a long perimeter would require prohibitive numbers of troops to provide depth everywhere. The problem is aggravated by the fact that restricted fields of fire prevent mutual support except from positions at intervals greatly reduced from those normal in open country.

95. Normally it will be better to accept some infiltration between localities and to forgo any attempt to hold a continuous line round the edge of a built-up area. Lines in depth can be pierced at selected points, and will rarely be within true supporting distance of each other, while a series of static strongpoints can be reduced piecemeal. It will be necessary, therefore, to concentrate on the defence of selected parts of a built-up area, such as the main routes into it and various key points which are well adapted for defence and which it is vital to deny to the enemy. These should be held as strong, independent, and self-supporting localities, each capable of all-round defence, each composed of mutually supporting blocks or houses, and each providing a pivot on which its mobile elements must be prepared to act offensively outside the area of the locality.

96. To ensure that subordinate commanders are clear as to the type of defence required of them, their responsibilities should be allotted specifically as *defended areas* or *defended localities*.

A commander is free to organize the defence of a *defended area* as he wishes and may permit penetration into the area with a view to entrapping the attackers. When allotted a *defended locality* a commander is restricted to the extent that he must prevent any degree of penetration from any direction; localities should, therefore, be of limited size. It will not be unusual for a subordinate commander to be allotted a defended area containing one or more defended localities within that area, but normally sub-units should be restricted to the defence of localities. Boundaries will be laid down between localities or areas to denote spheres of activity or limits for patrolling; they should not be along likely enemy lines of approach.

97. When the number of defenders is inadequate for the defence of a town allotted to him as a defended area the commander has alternative courses of action.

He may reduce the number of localities and areas and increase the strength of mobile reserves. He will thus ensure that the maximum use can be made of the forces at his disposal and that minimum numbers are locked up in localities that may not be affected by the fighting when it begins. Alternatively he may decide to disregard a part of the town and concentrate his defence in one selected area. A part of this area should lie on the perimeter of the town, to reduce the chances of encirclement and to allow for freedom of action outside it should occasion arise.

In the latter alternative the organization beforehand of parties to harass the enemy by guerilla methods in the part of the town that he does not intend to hold will help him in the defence of the remainder. He should try to arrange for the part of the town that he does not occupy to be shelled mercilessly as soon as the enemy enter it.

98. **Preparation.**—In any town there will be a wealth and variety of material and resources available for defensive measures. In order to use them to the best advantage and to deny their use to the enemy, careful planning will be necessary and a detailed order of priorities should be issued early on. The main difficulties will be to co-ordinate preparations and to ensure that no labour is wasted and that no work is omitted that can be done in the time available.

99. The main points requiring consideration when making preparations for defence will be :—

(a) In addition to tactical reconnaissance, the provision of reconnaissance parties to ascertain what material and resources are available.

(b) Liaison with civilian authorities concerning public services, transmission of information, arrangements for safeguarding of civilian population, use of police, provision of labour, medical assistance, etc.

(c) Traffic control and marking of routes and buildings.

(d) Collection and disposal of material.

(e) Preparation and issue of large scale plans or aerial photographs.

(f) Fire and air raid precautions.

(g) Preparation of main defences and obstacles, including the concealment of fire positions, snipers' posts, the erection of dummies, and the erection of really strong tank-proof barricades.

(h) Preparation of communications including the clearing of through ways in blocks of houses, the security of headquarters, and contact with troops outside.

(i) Preparation of alternative positions including likely positions for use by mobile reserves.

(j) The gaining of local knowledge of streets, routes, sewers, adjacent buildings and localities, etc. Orderlies must move through cover rather than along streets.

(k) Deception, ruses, booby traps, trip wires, self-raising alarms, electrified wire.

(*l*) Provision and storage of ammunition, supplies, water.
(*m*) Provision of latrines, their care and maintenance.
(*n*) Disposal of vehicles.
(*o*) Rehearsal of manning of alarm posts and temporary positions, and of counter-attacks.
(*p*) The medical layout, including ambulance posts, dressing stations, advanced surgical centres and hospital stores, as well as the care and inspection of water and all sanitation.

10. Conduct of the defence

100. **Offensive action.**—Streets and buildings are rigid ; a commander should be at pains to prevent them from imposing their rigidity on his dispositions, which must in all circumstances be highly flexible.

Flexibility will be greatly assisted if the defenders exploit to the full the advantage which will accrue from the thorough acquaintance of all ranks with the side-streets, alley-ways, passages, alternative ways into and out of buildings and compounds, etc., which abound in a built-up area. Complete local knowledge, which the attackers will not have, will give innumerable opportunities for moving reserves unseen, for ambushing or cutting off the enemy, and for arrangements which will prevent the enemy from turning the defences.

101. Although the defenders can remain concealed until the moment the enemy closes, the enemy will be able to exploit a similar advantage. It will be difficult to determine the weight and direction of attack or to secure and watch the flanks. Furthermore, owing to the difficulties of mutual support, an enemy may succeed in by-passing a locality or, particularly if an extensive area is held, in penetrating between strong points within a locality. Consequently reliance on static defence will be doomed to failure. The defence must be firm, yet mobile and aggressive. Such defence implies the use of a striking force and of firm bases from which mobile elements can operate. Battle outposts will be included in the initial stages.

102. *It must be the object of the defence not merely to repel an attack but to destroy as many of the enemy as possible.* If penetration is made between two localities, the defending garrisons must not only attempt to block further advance (which is merely to react to the enemy) but must exploit their superior knowledge of the ground to cut through and encircle as many of the attackers as possible. Abundant cover will enable the attackers to change direction, and their forward

elements will be difficult to locate ; but attack from a flank will afford the best opportunity of hitting the enemy hard, thus reducing the momentum of his attack, and of isolating and destroying him.

103. Tasks of striking force or main reserve.—The primary task will not be to provide the final defence against deep penetration. This force must be used in a mobile role, treating localities as strong bases for aggressive action. The main tasks, therefore, will be :—

(a) To cut off and destroy enemy penetration. On some occasions the enemy may be enticed forward, with this object in view.

(b) To restore a locality that has been overrun, by destroying the enemy in it.

104. It is most important to provide a mobile reserve, with the primary object of forming a striking force. This reserve may also have to hold a locality eventually. It should, therefore, have reconnoitred the positions which it may later be ordered to hold but will not normally hold a locality initially because there might be undue delay in concentrating the force from its positions, owing to the difficulty of centralized control in built-up areas.

It will often be best to provide two mobile reserves, each with a locality allotted as a secondary role. According to the direction of the attack, one will occupy its allotted locality, whilst the other remains available as the striking force ; it is, however, essential that the commander should make the decision on the respective roles sufficiently early to allow of the timely occupation of the locality which is to be defended.

105. Fighting patrols.—Darkness will favour the attacker, who must therefore be continuously harassed at night. Small active patrols must disorganize the enemy by every means—by stealth and ambush, and sometimes by deliberate noise—to such an extent that movement by him will be difficult and dangerous and that he cannot go far undetected.

It is, in fact, largely upon energetic and effective patrolling and sniping, both by day and by night, that the successful conduct of the defence depends.

The fighting value of a defensive garrison increases in proportion to the activity of its patrolling, which to a large extent deprives the attacker of the initiative, and enables effective defence to be maintained over a larger area. To allow the enemy to obtain superiority either in patrolling or in close-range sniping, is to court disaster.

106. **Alternative positions.**—The use of alternative positions is sometimes misunderstood. Their purpose is not to serve as a refuge when the garrison of a post or locality is hard pressed by the engaging enemy or is heavily bombarded.

Alternative positions are required for the following purposes :—
   (a) To meet necessary variations in day and night dispositions.
   (b) To meet the requirements of alternative tasks or a temporary change in role, e.g. to cover another area, to support a counter-attack, or to achieve surprise.
   (c) To mystify the enemy as to the position and strength of the defence, by occupying positions in rotation.
   (d) For occupation should a building, which forms a defended post, be burnt out.

107. *Defence of forward edges.*—There will be occasions when part of the defending garrison is sited on the forward edge of a built-up area ; its dispositions are liable to be pin-pointed, thus making the enemy's supporting fire for his attack very effective. It will then be advisable for the garrison to carry, out its harassing fire, before the enemy's main attack develops, from *temporary* positions. The eventual positions must be occupied in time to catch the assaulting enemy in the open.

CHAPTER IV—MINOR TACTICS AND METHODS

NOTE.—The methods described in Secs. **11** and **12** are intended as a guide and as a basis for training. They must be applied intelligently, the necessary modifications being made according to the type of building and to the situation in which the methods are used.

11. Section drill for clearing a house

108. Organization

(a) *Clearing group :—*
   Section commander.
   Bomber.
   First entry man.
   Second entry man.
   Look-out man.

When a large house is to be cleared, this group may be increased by withdrawing men from the covering group, platoon HQ, or another section.

(b) *Covering group* :—

The Bren group with the remainder of the riflemen under the section second-in-command.

109. Duties of covering group

(a) To cover all possible fire positions that command the approach of the clearing group.

(b) To cover as far as possible the flank exits, in order to prevent enemy movement to or from the house.

(c) To provide smoke and take deceptive measures as required.

110. Action by clearing group

(a) Section commander and bomber take up an intermediate position from which to direct and cover the entry men towards the point of entry.

(b) Entry men approach the point of entry at best speed according to cover available. Their means of entry will depend upon the type of defences, and may be either through an open door, window, or other aperture, or through a hole made by the use of suitable demolition equipment. At the last moment before entering a room it may be advisable to search it by fire (machine carbine, grenade, etc.) and follow up at top speed before any inmates have had time to recover.

(c) On gaining an entrance entry men get away quickly from the point of entry and stand with their backs to the wall covering the rest of the room and any doors.

(d) Section commander and bomber follow up entry men (as a result of observation or on signal from the latter).

(e) All four move out of the room in the order : section commander, bomber, first entry man, second entry man.

(f) The look-out man stays at the entry, watches for signals, and acts as guide, runner, etc., for liaison with the covering group and with platoon headquarters.

(g) The remainder aim at getting to the top of the house as quickly as possible, leaving the second entry man near the entrance of the room to cover any stairs and passages. This is the ideal method, but it will not be possible if the staircase is strongly defended or heavily obstructed.

(h) The covering group follow up and, if so ordered by the section commander, enter the house as soon as the entry group have successfully completed their entry. They will assist the second entry man in covering points from which the enemy may approach and, under the section second-in-command, will be prepared either to help in searching the house or to provide fire outside the house.

(*i*) The house is, if possible, searched downwards from the top, the first entry man opening the door of each room in turn, and providing protection against enemy approaches to the landing or head of the stairs. The section commander enters each room first at speed and turns quickly with his back to the wall. The bomber throws grenades as ordered by the section commander, and generally acts as the section commander's assistant and escort. If search from the top is not possible, it will proceed upwards floor by floor, using the ordinary methods of fire and movement, with the ground floor held as a relatively secure base for operations.

(*j*) The section commander reports, by word of mouth or signal, that the house is clear.

111. General notes.—Sometimes it will be expedient for the section commander and bomber to enter a house *before* the entry men, and as soon as the latter have prepared the way. Normally, however, the drill given above should be carried out, in order to ensure that the entry men will not be left waiting in the open, and because they will usually be in a better position to make a quick entry.

112. Search from the top downwards may induce the enemy to escape into the street, where he can be easily dealt with, whereas if driven upwards he is more likely to become desperate and show fight.

The difficulty of getting to the top of a building will be greatest when once the enemy has had time to recover from the first shock of assault. Up to, and immediately after, that moment he will, to a certain extent, be uncertain and concerned chiefly with what is happening outside the building ; consequently the greatest speed will be necessary, and the acceptance of some risk justified on the part of the clearing group, in order to get to the top as soon as possible, thereby avoiding the more hazardous operation of fighting their way upwards.

When houses are attached, or close together, it should be possible to enter an adjacent house via the roofs or party walls, using the methods of effecting an entry already described.

It is a golden rule never to stand in doorways, against doors, or anywhere on a floor except at the very edge, where movement cannot be accurately located from below.

12. Platoon drill for clearing occupied houses

113. **Plan.** (*See* diagram page 29).

No. 1 Section gives covering fire.

No. 2 Section assaults houses on right.

No. 3 Section assaults houses on left.

Platoon headquarters and reserve move forward one or two houses in rear of one of the leading sections. Part of platoon headquarters may assist No. 1 Section in giving covering fire.

Streets or back areas A and C are killing grounds and out of bounds to attackers. B may be used by attackers for speed of movement under overhead covering fire.

114. **Drill.**—Sequence of action.—*See table opposite.*

115. General notes

(*a*) The above drill is a guide only and may require variation and elaboration to suit circumstances. For example, in para. 114 (*c*) the covering group of No. 2 Section may be ordered to stay outside to cover either its own clearing group or No. 1 Section on to the next house, or to fire on any enemy who may try to escape from the house during the entry of the clearing group. Such methods will either require previous decision and inclusion in the initial orders, or will be left to the initiative of the covering group commander.

(*b*) At stage (*h*) the platoon commander may reverse the roles of No. 1 Section and one of the leading sections.

(*c*) If one of the leading sections is held up, the other section must continue the forward movement until the objective is reached.

(*d*) A platoon reserve, however small, will be useful in order that the platoon commander may have a force under his immediate control. It may consist of platoon HQ personnel only, or may be supplemented by one or two men withdrawn from rifle sections.

Platoon Drill for clearing occupied

	1 Section	2 Section
(a)	Siting of initial covering fire	
(b)	Covering fire	Clearing group assaults and clears HOUSE
(c)	ditto	Covering group follows up clearing group as soon as latter have entered house successfully
(d)	ditto	Section commander posts section to fire across on to HOUSE 2, and signals to Section as soon as this covering fire posted
(e)	ditto	Covering fire
(f)	ditto	ditto
(g)	ditto	ditto
(h)	Section moves forward as required to cover further advance of 2 and 3 Sections	2 and 3 Sections would moment when cover required further forward either continue and move of 1 Section 1 Section in position

[*To face page* 28]

s—Sequence of Action.

3 Section	Platoon HQ and reserve

ming up of assault sections.

vering fire	Covering fire and general direction of attack
ditto	ditto
ditto	ditto
earing group assaults and clears HOUSE 2	ditto
vering group follow up clearing group as soon as latter have entered house successfully	ditto
ction commander posts section to fire across to HOUSE 3, and signals to 2 Section as soon as covering fire is posted	ditto
ately as above until re from 1 Section is 2 and 3 Sections can ously with forward ver its move until	Follow in rear of either 2 or 3 Section when latter have reached (approximately) HOUSE 5 or 6

PLATOON BATTLE DRILL FOR CLEARING TWO ROWS OF OCCUPIED HOUSES

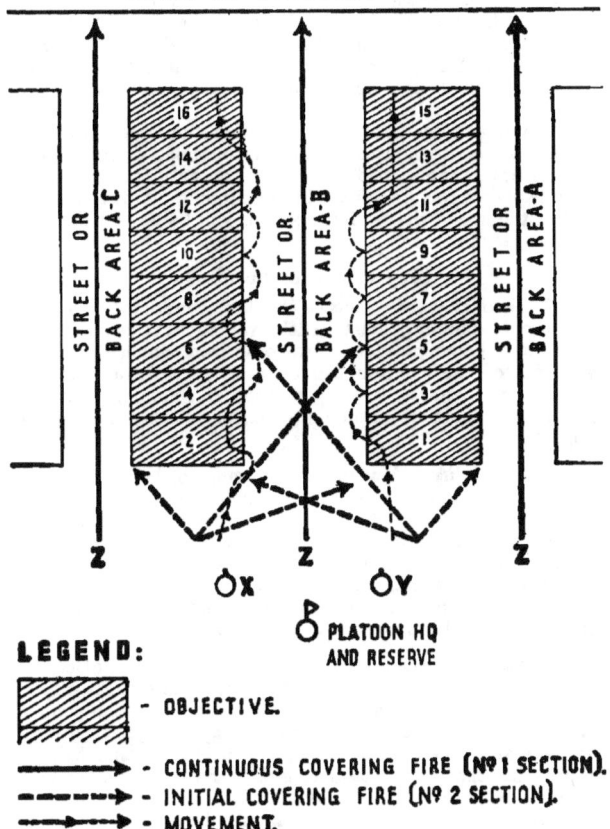

NOTES

(1) X represents No. 2 Section with clearing group ready to assault and covering group giving initial covering fire.

(2) Y represents No. 3 Section disposed similarly to No. 2 Section.

(3) No. 1 Section (Z) gives covering fire, possibly assisted by part of Platoon Headquarters.

(4) Platoon Headquarters and reserve follow either No. 2 or No. 3 Section.

116. *Alternative methods*—The two leading sections can advance up the *backs* of the two rows of houses (i.e. via entrances in A and C), when B would be the killing area. Alternatively, one row at a time may be taken on, when B might be the killing area, with the two leading sections leap-frogging through the houses and back gardens between A and B or C and B.

To approach by back ways is often the best method of gaining access to houses; and this method, where circumstances are suitable, also allows the concentration of a large volume of covering fire on the killing ground. A disadvantage is that the fire of the leading sections will be less effective for covering each other.

13. Defence of buildings

117. *Tactical requirements.*—The first consideration is that a house or building must satisfy the tactical requirements, which may be to provide a firm base from which the mobile elements of the garrison can operate, to withstand assault, to cover an obstacle, to support another building, to provide a link in a chain of communication, or to deny a particular approach.

118. *Durability.*—A very large number of bombs or shells are required to affect seriously a built-up area. The most durable buildings are those with steel or reinforced concrete frames; the next are those of stone construction. Brick buildings are very weak, while wooden buildings, once they have become a target, may be death traps.

The effect of fire upon a building should be considered and all non-essential inflammable material removed.

119. *Surroundings.*—Adequate fields of fire are, of course, essential in order that tactical offensive requirements may be met, but buildings must also be considered from the point of view of their own defence. A house may be rejected, even if half the area round it is flat and open, if the other half has approaches that are difficult to guard and therefore the more likely to be used by the enemy.

A house selected for defence should be inconspicuous—an advantage inherent in one of a row of houses—and should not be open to observation from a dominating feature.

Approaches to and from a building should be available out of view of the enemy.

Full use should be made of weapon slits sited at the edges of gardens. Such positions may be readily concealed from the air and are not liable to be buried if the buildings collapse. Moreover, beaten zone of LMGs sited at ground level is greater than when fired from the upper floors of a house. Alternative positions in the house should, however, be selected even if weapon slits can be sited outside.

120. *Defensive capabilities.*—Buildings, including their interiors and the roofs, must be capable of all-round defence. Their size and design, combined with the surroundings, will serve as a guide to the minimum strengths of garrisons.

121. There must be no distinction of place or person when a building is required for defensive purposes.

122. **Reconnaissance of a building.**—Points to look for are :—

- (a) Observation posts.
- (b) Fields of fire. Primarily these will be required to enable the garrison to carry out its main tasks. The actual defence of the building itself is a secondary consideration.
- (c) Extent to which loopholes are required.
- (d) Strength of building, and whether walls are bulletproof.
- (e) Entrances and exits ; too many will be a source of weakness, and will necessitate additional material and labour for blocking them up.
- (f) Communications with adjacent houses, and with fire posts in the garden and outhouses, if any.
- (g) Alternative positions.
- (h) Facilities for defence against bombing and artillery fire.
- (i) Water supply : for drinking and putting out fires.
- (j) Material and resources available in the building and in adjacent buildings.
- (k) Rough estimate of work and material required for putting building into state of defence.
- (l) Dressing station.
- (m) Cookhouse.
- (n) Latrines.

123. **Local protection.**—This should be considered for both the outside and inside of a building, and with the different conditions of day and night in mind.

(a) *Outside a building.*—By day, and sometimes by night, one or two positions outside a building may afford better protection than inside and may prevent the enemy getting near enough to neutralize the defences in the building itself.

Sentries should be posted outside a building whenever possible, especially by night. They should be on ground level, and on the roof if the latter is accessible to the enemy. From the outside they will be in a better position than from inside a building to listen for and investigate any movement. By night additional protection will be required in the form of small active patrols. These may be found by the combined garrisons of buildings within a particular area.

Obstacles, either wire, barricades, mines, or booby traps, should be placed round the house itself and at likely approaches.

Shelter and weapon slits should be dug for protection against bombing and as possible alternative positions.

Fields of fire should be cleared, and dummy positions might be erected in suitable places to attract the enemy and influence his choice of lines of advance.

(b) *Inside a building and on the roof*

    i. *Material protection* in the form of sandbags, mattresses, earth-filled cupboards, chests-of-drawers, etc., will be required for providing additional protection where walls, particularly those in which loop-holes have been made, and floors are not bullet-proof.

   ii. All accessible entrances should be barricaded, except those intentionally left open as traps and those required for use by the garrison, which should be specially prepared for blocking at short notice.

       Staircases, and sometimes passages, may require blocking. Many devices can be thought out for this purpose; a short coil of concertina wire, coupled with the removal of a section of the bannisters, is an effective method for stairs.

  iii. Communications from the roof and within the house must be considered. If time permits, alternative means of passing from room to room, or floor to floor, other than by the staircase, should be made, provided that the structure of the building is not seriously weakened. If cellars are used they should have two exits.

  iv. *Shoring up* of rooms, especially cellars and ground-floor rooms, may be necessary, to withstand the additional weight of sandbags and protective material, and the blast effect of explosions.

       The main points to be borne in mind are that the floors must be sufficiently strong to take the extra pressure; that shoring timbers must be strong and vertical and must rest on a solid base; that boards or planks must be inserted between the top of the timbers and solid portions of the ceiling; and that wedges, when driven between a baseplate and the bottom end of a shoring timber, take up the strain sufficiently without lifting the ceiling construction above.

v. Provision of water, sand, and implements for dealing with an outbreak of fire is necessary. All baths, basins, and buckets should be kept full against burst mains or fire. Gas and electric light should be turned off at the main to guard against the risks of fire and of lights being accidentally turned on. Inflammable material not required should be removed.

vi. In considering the gas-proofing of a room, it should be borne in mind that, though this will be useful at headquarters, signal offices, and dressing stations, the presence of a gas-proof room will tend to restrict the inquisitiveness and alertness of a garrison. Normally, protection afforded by the respirator will be sufficient.

14. Siting of weapons

124. For the defence of the building itself automatic weapons should, as a general rule, be sited near ground level, with rifles and hand-thrown grenades at first floor level or higher.

Alternative positions should be provided so that fire can be switched as required. In the final stages of an assault rifles should normally be used for the longer fields of fire, and automatics for the short restricted fields of fire that the enemy are more likely to rush. Weapons will be disposed with the enemy's probable lines of approach in mind.

All weapons should be used as far back from a window, loophole, or other aperture as is possible, consistent with their fields of fire having sufficient width and depth.

It is erroneous to think that rifles and automatics should, where practicable, be sited to fire left-handed from a window in preference to right-handed because of the firer presenting a smaller target. In practice the firer presents a smaller target when firing to the right, provided that he uses the inside of the wall as cover and that his weapon is not required to project outside the window.

125. **Windows and loopholes.**—Sufficient windows and loopholes are required for alternative positions, but the number of loopholes should be kept as low as possible because they weaken the structure of the building and involve labour and

material. Loopholes, especially those for observation, should be made in unexpected places such as under a window sill or through the tiles of a roof.

126. The following considerations should be borne in mind :—
- (a) To obtain a wide arc, loopholes are often made in the form of rectangular slits. They are, however, more effective if shaped like a V with the wider section on the inside. Since they are also likely to be used for firing at targets above and below, they should be roughly cone shaped to present as small an exterior aperture as possible.
- (b) The edges of a loophole, especially when made in brickwork, will be liable to splinter when hit by a bullet. If possible, a protective lining, e.g. sacking held in place by wire netting, should be installed to reduce splinter effect. For the same reason sandbags nearest to the firer or observer should be filled with earth or sand, and not shingle or stones.
- (c) When not in use a loophole or window requires some form of cover, bullet-proof if possible, that can be placed in position to prevent the enemy seeing or firing through it.
- (d) The glass of all windows should be removed from a defended house and from adjacent houses in the vicinity.
- (e) Methods of concealment and deception include making dummy loopholes indistinguishable from the real ones ; painting or draping well-known and likely objects against or round loopholes ; use of lace curtains ; and placing of dummy figures at apertures not in use.
- (f) When using a window, a firer should normally have a kneeling or standing position prepared on either side of the window and protected by the wall. As he will require to fire downwards, these positions should be raised well above the level of the sill upon a table or similar object, and sufficiently far away to prevent his rifle protruding through the window. A lying position does not always allow sufficient freedom for firing at widely varying angles, especially in elevation.
- (g) Some loopholes should be made inside the building in case the enemy should break in. Holes in floors will enable grenades to be thrown from an upper room into the one below. If enlarged, they also provide alternative communication between rooms on different levels.

(h) Wire netting or similar material over windows and loopholes, especially those near ground level, serves to keep out hand-thrown grenades. The wire should hang or be fastened below the outside sill to prevent any missile lodging on the sill. A small gap or overlapping slit should be made to allow grenades to be thrown out or a firer to lean out if necessary.

(j) Care should be taken to prevent smoke by day, and artificial light by night, being seen through a loophole or window from the outside. A screen should be provided between the head of the man at the loophole or window and the source of light.

(k) Loopholes at ground level, e.g. when using the grating from a cellar, should have a small shelving trench dug below them on the outside. The object is to catch grenades that roll towards the base of the wall or drop after hitting the wall above and to cause them to explode below the level of the loophole.

(l) It may be necessary, in order to give adequate protection, for some of the ground-floor windows not required for defence purposes to be blocked up and made bullet-proof. Boards with earth or shingle between them will be effective. The practice, however may indicate to the enemy that a given house is occupied.

(m) Observation in all directions must be arranged. A loophole covered with appropriately painted wire gauze from the meat safe permits an observer to see without being seen.

15. Do's and don'ts

127. Shots must be accurate to pierce loopholes and slits ; therefore fire one deliberate shot or burst rather than two or three hurried ones. Exceptions will be when you are " browning " the enemy through a wall, floor, or ceiling, or when taking a quick snap shot on the move.

128. Because of short ranges and ample cover, shift your position frequently, provided always that you can carry out the tasks allotted. Crawl or worm about, always keeping as low down as possible.

129. Move into a firing or observing position slowly. Quick movement catches the eye more easily. In looking round the

corner of a house or street it may pay to do so at ground level and not at ordinary height. The enemy will expect you to look round at standing height, and at this height the shoulder and side of the body become visible as well as the head.

130. Always have prepared in your own mind what to do in event of emergency ; cover is abundant, but actions are short and sudden. This rule applies also to the men under your command. Let them know beforehand what action is required in different eventualities or if things go wrong, e.g. where to go, which way, methods of retaliation, etc.

131. Be practised in " reading " buildings and their surroundings and taking in probable points of enemy fire. The results will help to guide your actions, and the more likely points can be checked up with binoculars, by men detailed to watch particular ones, by simulated movement, or by deliberately drawing fire.

132. Use methods of distraction. Before entering an occupied room, crossing a street, or going up stairs, make a noise or throw an object to distract an enemy's attention elsewhere for that moment of time necessary to enable you to move first.

133. Don't put an observer, if possible, in a room alongside a firer. Noise deadens perception, and prevents the use of the ears for aiding visual observation.

134. Explosions and firing cause dense clouds of brick dust, etc. When preparing a building for defence, try to remove or cover over all unwanted objects that might cause dust clouds. The removal of plaster from walls will help. It will be advisable to keep loopholes damp to prevent dust from rising.

135. When crossing the top of a wall or similar crest, slide over face downwards, keeping the body as near the horizontal as possible.

136. Don't jabber when in action. It disconcerts your own side, and makes a silently working enemy appear more grimly efficient. At the right moment the voice can be invaluable for spurring men on and letting them know where you are or what is happening, or for deceiving the enemy as to your intentions and strength.

137. In an occupied room a useful precaution is to have a table handy for use as a protective and movable screen in an

emergency. It should have additional protection, such as a mattress fixed to the table top, the table being placed on its side.

138. When smoke is used don't stint the volume. An inadequate smoke screen is almost useless.

139. Withhold your fire until the psychological moment; think in terms of entrapping the enemy, not merely repelling him.

140. Overcome any disinclination to " wreck a place "; use anything and everything you want, if it helps to defeat the enemy.

141. Examine your building from the enemy's viewpoint, when time permits, to see that nothing tells a tale. This reconnaissance will also give some idea of the probable line of advance by the enemy.

CHAPTER V—TRAINING

16. Object

142. Training for fighting in built-up areas must be directed largely to the development, by means of demonstration, lecture, and practice, of confidence in the use of special methods involved. Each individual must feel not only that he is an expert in such areas, but also that he is certain that the men and sub-units alongside him are equally expert and can be depended upon to do their job in the actual fighting, although perhaps out of sight and hearing of himself and of each other.

17. Methods

143. *Ground.*—Normally realistic ground is easily obtained, especially in " blitzed " areas. For elementary training a great deal of use can be made of a single house, but at least a small built-up area, including a street, is required for more advanced training, in order to allow those being trained to get used to the feeling of moving in, around, and over buildings for purposes other than those to which they have been accustomed.

144. *Lectures.*—Much of the subject matter can be explained in the form of diagrams. Short lectures serve as a useful means of introduction to demonstrations and for working up interest.

145. *Demonstrations.*—These are particularly suitable for this form of training, and can cover almost all its aspects. The area required to stage a demonstration can be small, and yet, given good preparation and a sense of showmanship, a demonstration offers scope for many valuable lessons.

146. *Models.*—Built-up areas can be realistically and easily portrayed by means of sand table models, dolls' houses, etc.

147. *Vertical photographs.*—Useful for conducting indoor exercises and for discussions. Used as stereoscopic pairs they bring out clearly many characteristics of built-up areas.

148. *Exercises.*—Whether conducted for individuals or teams, the provision of an enemy and battle noises makes for realism.

The enemy should be carefully controlled to avoid an undue number of clashes and to simplify umpiring. The local Home Guard might act as defenders of a street, and because of their local knowledge, form a worthy enemy from whom much can often be learned.

For smaller exercises those not taking part can learn much by acting as critics. TEWTs for officers and NCOs will be of great value.

18. Stages

149. *Elementary training.*—The start of training should be devoted principally to introducing the individual to this particular type of ground ; to teaching him its characteristics ; to increasing his probably vague knowledge of items such as types of walls, drains, manholes, cock-lofts, eaves, roofs, shafts, cellars, and what is found between a ceiling and the floorboards above ; to practise him in movement both by day and by night ; and generally to making him regard a built-up area as a potential fighting ground as opposed to an area that provides shelter and comforts.

150. *Advanced individual training.*—This stage should include the finer points in use of weapons and explosives, the recognition and location of fire, agility, stealthy movement and bold, rapid movement, the selection of positions and use of cover, observation, and the preparation of a house for defence.

151. *Teamwork.*—To include the teaching of battle drills, patrol work, and generally the welding of individuals into teams.

APPENDIX A

PROTECTION TABLE

Safe thickness in inches against armour-piercing LMG fire up to 7·92 millimetres (burst of 20 rounds) or splinters from a 100-lb. HE bomb bursting not less than 30 ft away.

Serial No.	Material	Safe thickness in inches	Remarks
1	Earth or loam as in parapets	60	
2	Chalk as in parapets	60	Variable
3	Clay as in parapets	72	Variable
4	Sand, loose or between boards	30	
5	Brick rubble confined between boards	18	
6	Coal between boards	24	
7	Road metal (1½ in–2 in) between boards	14	
8	Sandbags filled with :—		
	(a) Rubble	30	
	(b) Earth	30	
	(c) Road metal	20	
	(d) Shingle	20	
	(e) Sand	30	
9	Brickwork in lime mortar	18	
10	Concrete, unreinforced	12	
11	Mild steel plate	1¾	
12	Timber	60	Variable

APPENDIX B

METHODS OF SCALING WALLS

1. Equipment

1. Some of the following methods involve the use of a service rifle. Where possible a similar object should be used instead to obviate the risk of a rifle becoming damaged through such treatment and thereby becoming useless to its

owner. Service rifles will not be used for these purposes in training, except for demonstrating methods—and then only after they have been suitably protected.

2. *Toggle ropes*.—These consist of lengths of rope, of about 6 ft, each with a " toggle " or short wooden bar at one end and an eye or loop at the other, both firmly spliced into the rope. They can be put to a variety of uses, either singly, in pairs, or joined together.

3. *Rifle slings joined together by the D's* may sometimes be used in place of toggle ropes.

2. Methods

4. **Double rope haul** (14 ft with single length toggle ropes)—Used when two men of a party are already on top of a wall or at a window above the ground floor of a house :—
- (a) Two men at the window or on top of the wall each unsling a length of toggle rope (or ropes) and lower them down, toggle first.
- (b) A man at the bottom grasps a toggle in each hand and, facing the wall, places a foot against the base of the wall about 3 ft up.
- (c) On the word " haul " by the man at the bottom, the two men at the window haul in the rope and the man at the bottom walks up the wall.

5. **Rifle haul** (10 ft)

Similar to the above but a rifle is used instead of a rope.

6. **Single hoist** (10 ft)

(a) One man crouches with his back to the wall and places his hands, interlocked and palms uppermost, on one knee.

(b) Another man advances towards him, places one foot in the cupped hands, and springs upwards.

(c) At the same time he is lifted upwards by the man against the wall.

7. **Double hoist** (12 ft)

(a) Two men, Nos. 1 and 2, crouch against a wall facing towards each other. Each interlocks his hands, palms uppermost, thus forming two steps about 9 in from the wall.

(b) No. 3 man places his hands against the wall and a foot on each step.

(c) On No. 3 giving the word " heave " Nos. 1 and 2 heave him up the wall. No. 3 grasps the top and hauls himself up.

8. Rifle butt (15 ft)

(*a*) Three men stand at the foot of a wall, No. 1 with weapons slung, Nos. 2 and 3 with rifles carried.

No. 1 stands against the wall with his left knee raised.

(*b*) No. 2 places butt of rifle under No. 1's left foot (the toe of the butt should be placed against the wall).

(*c*) No. 1 puts weight on left foot and lifts right foot.

(*d*) No. 3 puts rifle butt under right foot, No. 1 takes his weight on right foot, lifts left foot, and so on until he can grasp the top of the wall and haul himself up.

9. Human pyramid (12 ft)

(*a*) Three men put their arms round each others waists and " scrum down " against the wall.

(*b*) No. 4 places himself close behind them on his hands and knees facing a flank.

(*c*) No. 5 climbs on the backs of two of the first three men ; and gets on hands and knees facing a flank. He leaves the third back clear to act as a step.

(*d*) Three steps are formed for a man to walk up.

10. Ladder (11–12 ft)

(*a*) Two men are needed, with two rifles or poles about 4 ft long.

(*b*) These men take up position close to the wall, facing each other, and kneeling, place one rung across the outer knees and the other rung across the shoulders nearest the wall.

(*c*) The climber uses the rungs as steps and, standing on the top rung, can either spring or be lifted as the kneelers stand up, until he is able to reach the top of the wall.

(*d*) This method can be used for crossing wire, when it is necessary to run up the steps and jump.

(*e*) Extra height can be obtained when scaling a wall by a second pair of men standing immediately next to the wall supporting a rifle or pole at the full extent of their arms.

APPENDIX C

USE OF EXPLOSIVES IN BUILT-UP AREAS
General

1. The uses for explosives which will be more common in fighting in built-up areas than in other types of warfare are :—

    (*a*) Demolition of girders and pillars of brickwork or masonry with the purpose of causing a building to collapse. Guncotton slabs (1 lb) or No. 75 grenades form useful cutting charges for this purpose.

(b) Breaching of walls to improve internal communications within buildings or blocks of buildings, or to force an entrance into a building or from one room to another. This is sometimes known as "mouseholing".

(c) Destruction of, or forcing an entrance into, strongpoints by the use of pole charges.

Demolition by cutting charges

2. When using guncotton slabs or No. 75 grenades, the following points should be noted :—

(a) The charge must extend across the full breadth of the object to be destroyed.

(b) The charge must be in close contact with the surface of the object to be demolished. Voids between the slabs (or grenades) should be packed with clay.

(c) To ensure complete detonation, slabs (or grenades) must be in close contact with one another. If they are not, each separate charge must have its own point of detonation, the charges being fired simultaneously by means of detonating fuze.

(d) With guncotton slabs the minimum charge is one slab per six inches run of structure against which they are being used. Such a charge will cut a thickness of one inch of steel or two feet of brickwork or masonry.

The No. 75 grenade contains $1\frac{1}{2}$ lbs. of explosive and is, therefore, slightly more powerful.

Breaching of walls

3. The following charges are likely to be effective against brickwork :—

(a) One No. 75 grenade or guncotton slab against a thickness of $4\frac{1}{2}$ inches.

(b) Two grenades or slabs against a thickness of 9 inches.

(c) Three grenades or four slabs against a thickness of $13\frac{1}{2}$ inches. The grenades are preferable.

4. Battering will usually be necessary to enlarge the hole to enable a man to get through. If no heavier or more suitable implement is available, the rifle butt will serve.

5. A good method is by the use of two separate slabs or grenades fired simultaneously.

6. The effect of the dust and smoke caused by the explosion

in the inner room is sufficient to prevent any immediate retaliatory action against a man passing through the hole.

If battering or a second charge is required, a No. 69 grenade lobbed through the hole should be enough to keep the next room clear.

7. The blast effect of the No. 75 grenade may affect walls other than those attacked, particularly $4\frac{1}{2}$-inch partition walls in rooms with few, or small, windows and doors.

8. In any case, attackers should retire to put at least one wall, and preferably two, between them and the charge. "Mouse-holing" should not be attempted with our own troops in an immediately flanking room.

Pole charges

9. Guncotton slabs or No. 75 grenades can be used. Two battens about 3 feet long are lashed together diagonally and charges tied to the ends of both upper arms, which should be about 2 and $1\frac{1}{2}$ feet apart respectively for grenades and slabs. The lashed battens carrying the charges are propped against the wall, so that the charges fit flush against it.

This form of pole charge will effectively breach brick walls up to 18 inches thick.

10. A heavier type consists of a wooden box, containing the charge, mounted on the end of a pole. The pole is used to place the charge in position, and as a strut to hold it in place. The size of the box will depend on the charge required.

A pole charge of this type is suitable for attacking the loophole of a pill-box but is not effective against thick reinforced concrete walls.

Miscellaneous charges

11. No. 74 grenades ("Sticky Bombs") are useful for making breaches in brick walls. They are ineffective against stone-built walls or houses. As they will not stick to dusty brickwork, a platform about 2 ft. 6 in. high must be constructed. Two grenades will make a hole in a 14-inch brick wall large enough to permit a man to enter. They should be banged against the wall so as to ensure that the flask breaks and to obtain as large an area of contact as possible. Only the second grenade should be primed.

12. No. 68 anti-tank grenades have a good drilling effect on brickwork up to 14 inches thick and make a hole of about 9 inches diameter.

13. Anti-tank mines, Marks IV and V, can be initiated with a primer, detonator and safety fuze. The primer is inserted into the fuze socket of the mine. If good contact is obtained the result is excellent, but the mines are difficult to fire and awkward to handle. They are waterproof and small arms fire will not detonate them. Mines can also be fired by a No. 36 Mills grenade, but this method gives only four seconds for the attackers to get under cover, and adequate protection from the fragments is necessary.

APPENDIX D

PLATES

The following plates show characteristic layouts of towns. They may be used in conjunction with an epidiascope and screen, and for discussing and setting problems of attack and defence.

NOTE.—Scale of Plates Nos. 1 to 6 is 1 : 50,000.

Contour interval 10 metres.

PLATE 1

Example of a dense built up area. Showing the various stages of clusters of houses and open spaces, detached and semi-detached houses, and large central blocks.

PLATE 2

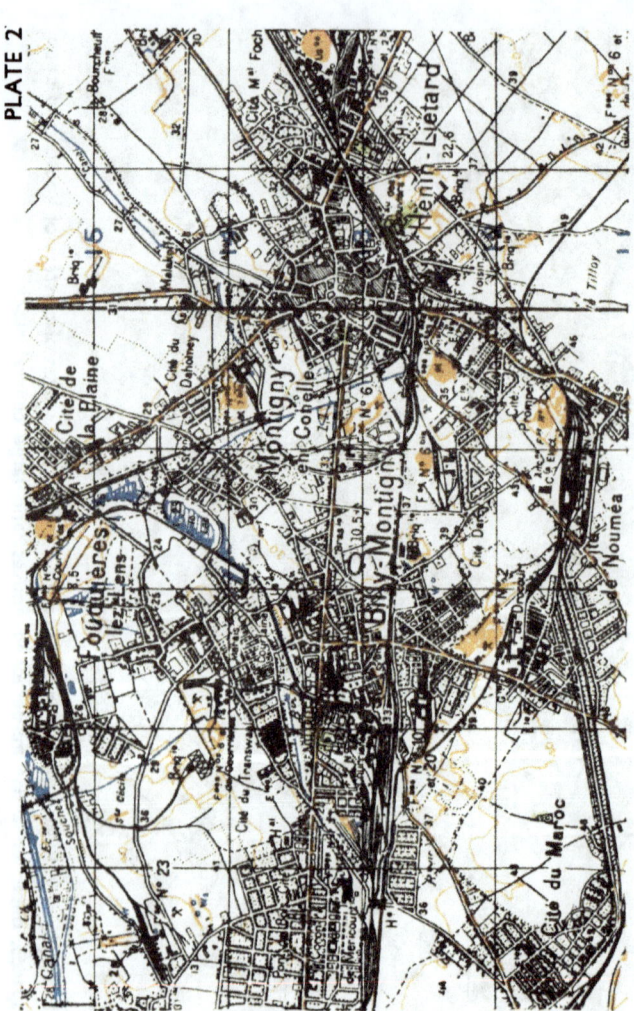

Example of an open built up area with an extensive and obscure perimeter.
Note: Features marked in red are slag heaps.

PLATE 3

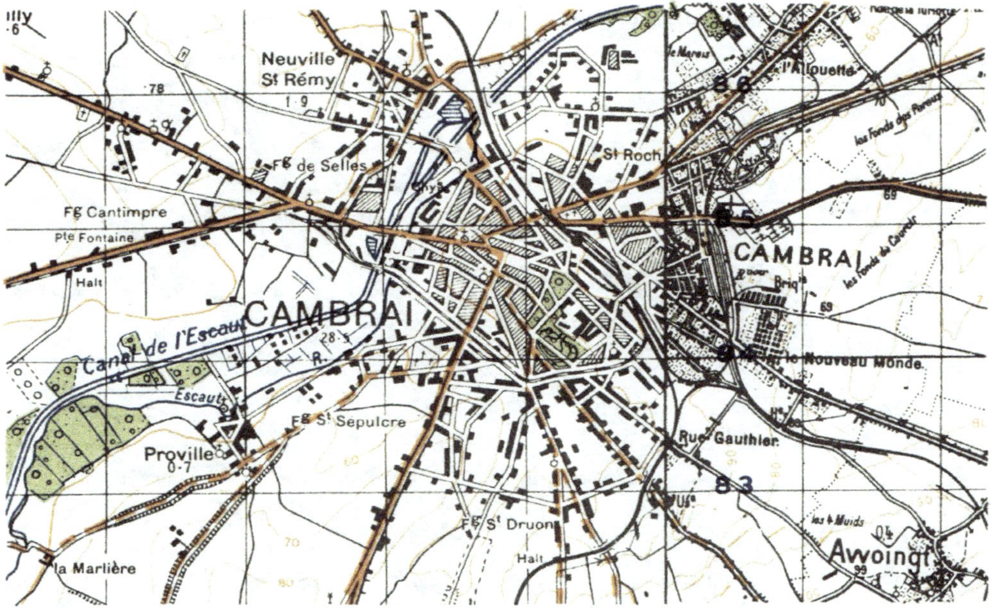

Example of town with marked ribbon development.
Note : Small streets in centre of town are omitted.

PLATE 4

Example of town with clearly defined inner perimeter. The layout provides many possibilities for defence.

PLATE 5

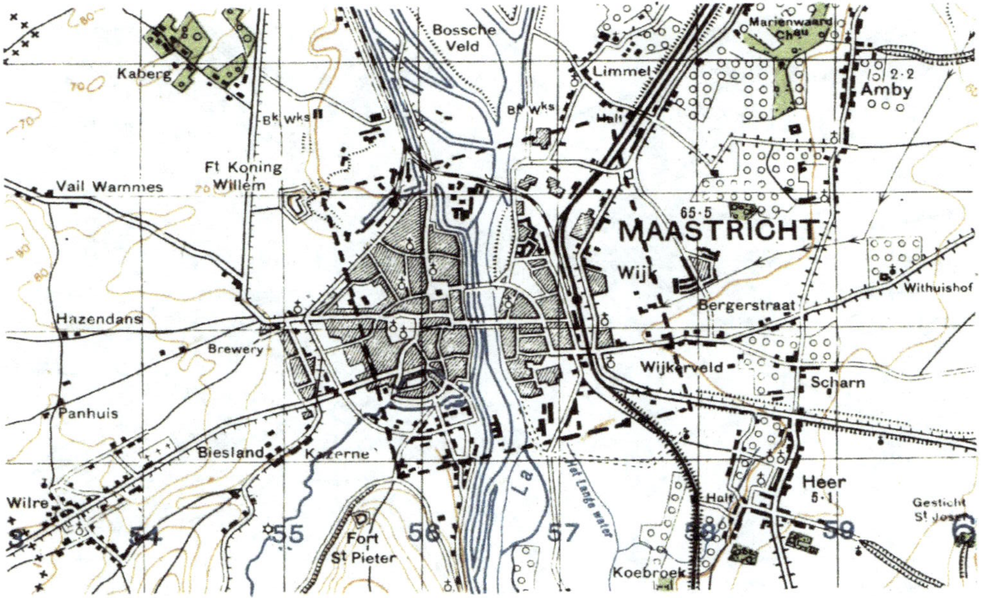

Old fortress town with clearly defined perimeter. (See Plate 1f).

PLATE 6

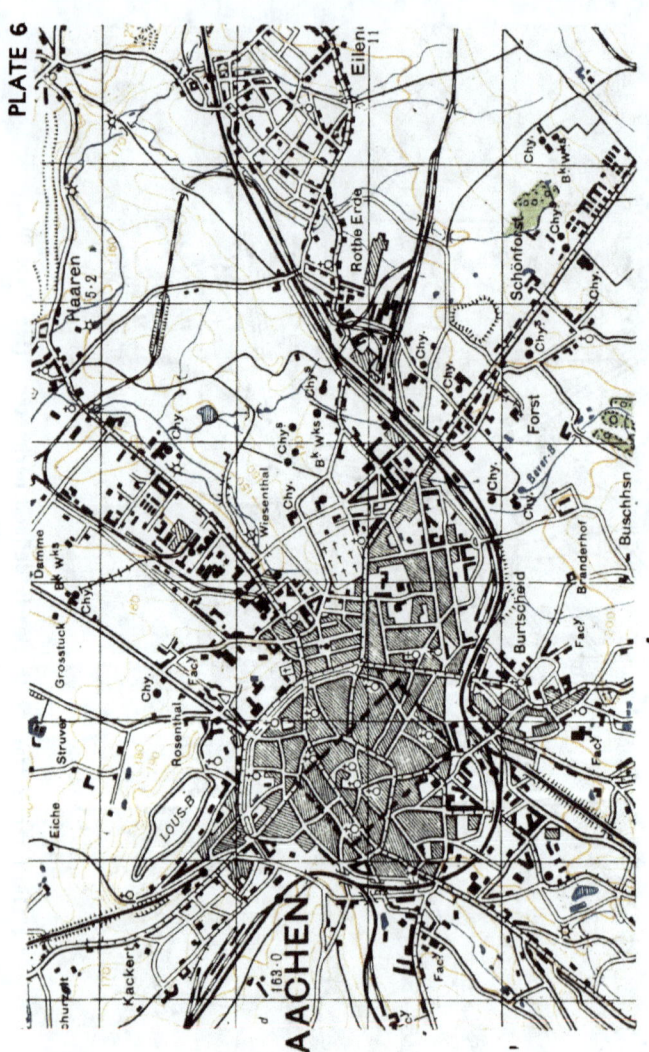

Marked area approximates to Plate 7.

PLATE 7

AACHEN
Typical lay-out near the centre of a large town. Areas of bomb damage are marked by dotted lines.

PLATE 8

MAINZ
An area in which the roof factor does not predominate to the extent which it did originally, and where ability to scale walls will be of increased importance.

PLATE 9

HAMBURG
Example of blocks near the centre of a town, showing wells within each block.

PLATE 10

DUSSELDORF
A high proportion of roof area compared with the total area, showing the importance of commanding the roof tops in this instance.

PLATE 11

MAASTRICHT

Possible scale of vertical photographs on which commanders and staff may be required to work. Note the proportion of streets which do not run in straight lines.

[For map *see* PLATE 5.]

www.ingramcontent.com/pod-product-compliance
Lightning Source LLC
LaVergne TN
LVHW021120080426
835510LV00012B/1777